Faith,
Hope & Love

Faith, Hope & Love

Poems Of Inspiration
By

Doris Washington

Book Cover & Photographs By Joni Meyers

Library of Congress Control Number: 2008901591
ISBN: Hardcover   978-1-4363-2417-5
                 Softcover   978-1-4363-2416-8

This book was printed in the United States of America.

To order additional copies of this book, contact:
Xlibris Corporation
1-888-795-4274
www.Xlibris.com
Orders@Xlibris.com
47993

CONTENTS

AVENUES

THE BEAUTY OF LOVE

COULD YOU SING A SONG FOR THEM?

HOPE

BLESSINGS

Dedication

I dedicate this book in fond memory of my father William Buchanan Sr. *I have so many wonderful memories of so many things when you were in my life—You were a beacon of life.*

I would also like to give special thanks to my mother Emma Buchanan. For without her love and support, this work would not have been possible.

Mother, Thank you for so much.

Mother

*You've shown me how to be strong through life's trials
from day to day.
You've shown me that patience is learned through time,
and to welcome life's challenges as they come my way.*

*You've shown me that people love differently in their own way.
This I've come to see.
And most of all-
You've shown me what a Mother is supposed to be.*

Acknowledgements

I would like to give special thanks to those persons who believed in me. To my loving husband John, my dear son John, my dear friends Priscilla Gallegos, Marilyn Donely, Kevin Pothier, and Barbara Roopnaraine of Bowie State University, Brittiney Dearing, Diane Jemison, Steve Kearney, my co—workers, many friends and family. Thank you for your encouragement and support. You helped make this piece of work all possible.

And I would like to give special thanks to my dear friend Joni Meyers for all your time and effort.

Foreword

Through our vast changing world today, I've found there is a great need for inspiration in our daily lives. I share with you my thoughts about keeping the faith, and the hope through the challenges of life, believing tomorrow will be the promise all will be brighter than you can ever imagine. And to remember with God's Grace, the world can be a most beautiful place as you hold on to the blessings.

My son John is my inspiration. Because of John, my first collection of poems *A Blessing, Caring & Sharing* was born. And I am happy to do another collection of poems I hope will inspire, and touch many lives. As a mother who lives with Autism, I've had my own share of hardship, and challenges. My hope in time there will be a great awareness about autism that would encourage us to discover all our children's gifts, and uniqueness.

I Thank God for the many blessings he grants me each day. I have a wonderful husband whose love and support has just been a blessing. I have a son whose own uniqueness is to love him as he is. I believe as we walk through this life to always keep the faith through every situation, hold on to hope, and carry the love wherever we go, then we can began to see the true beauty of living life. I give you *Faith, Hope & Love.*

Avenues

*Let your journey through life encourage you to hope,
to dream, and to be inspired.*

As I Plant The Seeds Of My Garden

As I Plant the Seeds of My Garden,
I plant my goals, my dreams,
And my visions of all I wish to do.
I cultivate the many goals,
I work towards to pursue.

As I Plant the Seeds of My Garden,
I vision my dreams blossoming with
Many opportunities.
And with self-determination,
My visions become a reality.

As I Plant the Seeds of My Garden,
I'm learning in accomplishing great
Achievements,
And Success,
Comes Courage,
And the belief in You!

I plant my goals,
My dreams,
And my visions.
Making them possible to become true.
As I Plant The Seeds Of My Garden.

Familiar

As I travel on this Journey of mine.
There're many doors to open,
and I'm confronted
with a place I once knew.
Knowing I can't go back.
For there're things I must do.

In order for me to grow,
What was,
I must move on,
and let go.
And as I open many doors I see
the places where I need to be.
Leaving what is-
Familiar

Believe In You

As you start a new phase in your life,
Just let go.
Go forward with a new vision always with Hope.
Stay encouraged no matter your challenges.
What is past is past.
Follow your dreams.
For each step you take is a step to where
you are to be.
For if you believe it.
All you wish for can come true.
Just-
Believe In You!

Loving You

Have love for others,
Give the best of you.
Stand up for what you believe in,
Just remain true.

Don't be persuaded by others
to change who you are.
Find your gift,
Learn to fly,
And you'll go far.

For life's greatest gift
is to believe in what you can do.
Knowing you have something
that is only unique to you.
For It Is All About-
Loving You!

The Comfort Zone

Great achievements does not come easy.
Sometimes you have to venture out
of the Comfort Zone.

The journey may seem long,
And you may wonder the dreams you set
will come to surface.

Oh! The comfort zone where all is good
and comfortable—why should one leave
chasing rainbows?

But that's the joy of it all.
Visualizing your dreams to come true.
Visualizing what you can achieve,
If you only believe,
And keep going
with the persistence,
and faith.
And your dreams can come true.
Leaving-
The Comfort Zone

Mountain

As you dream your dreams for self,
You can make it happen.
Yes, you can!

Move forward,
And turn the disappointments
Around with a positive attitude.
With a positive attitude,
You'll get results.

Trust in God always.
Let Him guide you every step you take.
Let Him guide you.

Go forward with Faith.
And no matter what's around,
Release those negative thoughts.

As you dream your dreams for self,
You can make it happen.
Yes, you can!

Just let go!
Move that-
Mountain!

To Fly Like An Eagle

To fly like an eagle
is to follow one's dreams
for however long it takes you.
Always daring about new adventures beyond
your imagination.

To fly like an eagle
is never giving up when the distance
seems so far.
Moving beyond the barriers, the obstacles.
Stead fast with self-determination.

To fly like an eagle
is to believe you can do all you dream to be.
Keeping your spirits high with positive energy,
Always giving your best!

To fly like an eagle
is believing each step you take,
Brings you closer that all is possible,
Beyond and Beyond!
Just Fly Like An Eagle!

Winners

Winners see beyond the boundaries,
Always searching high.
Winners always say: "I can do it"-
Believing their dreams can come true.
Winners never quit.
They stay the distance all through the end.
Winners don't compare themselves to others.
Only strive for the best in themselves.
Winners live by courage, and faith,
Standing tall with a job well done.
Winners see beyond the boundaries,
Always searching high.
Shining beautiful like a Star!

Beginnings

Circumstances can change,
And as one moves on,
A new day begins.

Moving on with no fears,
No worries of what's ahead.
Just confidence and peace of mind
To know it will be alright.

Going forward,
Moving beyond where you are,
To where you need to be.
For each step you take with Faith,
Believe your dreams can come true.
And it's just the-
Beginning!

Start Anew

When you start anew,
Just remember to keep you.
For each situation you journey is different.
And each one you meet is not the same.
Go into each experience leaving issues
Of the heart behind.
Let positive thoughts fill your mind.
Forgive, even if it's hard to do.
And just let Love take you,
When you-
Start Anew

Obstacles

You can't change yesterday,
You can change Today.
And tomorrow there'll always be Hope.
There'll be bridges to cross.
There'll be storms to get through.
And those obstacles will come when you least expect.
The good news is-
As you keep going, and believing,
You can do anything you set your heart to do.
With the Faith,
Your dreams can surface at anytime.
Just Keep Going!
Just Keep Believing!

Avenues

Alone I walk in the morning sun,
I find there're many roads to venture to.
Not sure where I'm going,
For there're many directions
to follow through.

With so much before me,
I find things can change
from one minute to the next.
And I'm learning life
is all about passing the test.

I ask the Lord to be my teacher.
I ask the Lord to be my guide.
And no matter what my life may be-
I feel His Love inside.

Alone I walk in the morning sun,
I find there're many roads to venture to.
Not sure where I'm going,
For there're many directions
to follow through.
There Are Many-
Avenues

A Journey Of A Thousand Steps

You must never give up when it seems so far.
You must never doubt when it all seems it's going nowhere.
You must never say you can't-always say you can.
It doesn't matter how long the journey.
What matters that you give it your all,
All the way to the end.
A true winner never gives up,
Never doubts when things go wrong,
Always gearing with positive energy,
No matter how the road turns.
For one single step leads to a thousand steps,
Making dreams come true.

The Beauty Of Love

Understanding, forgiveness, and compassion opens the heart to love.

A Friend

Friends may come and go.
And there're many acquaintances
you may come to know.
But remember to keep in mind.
A Friend will be there, come "rain or shine."
A Friend makes the time to hear a "hello", "how are you?"
And "I need to talk to you."
A Friend will also be honest—never cruel.

And when rumors arise,
And gossip feels the air.
A Friend will not listen to
hearsay of a friend—here or—there.

A Friend will love you for who you are.
A Friend will be a friend—near or far.
A Friend will forgive, even when you
let them down.
A Friend will wear a smile when you
wear a frown.
And when you are ready to give up on you,
A Friend will stay in your corner and carry
you through.

A Friend will make more room for talking and less
room for argument.
A Friend will not belittle, but offer encouragement.

A Friend will offer you their hand when the burdens
are heavy to bare.
A Friend will be thoughtful, and understanding.
For a friend who is true—will always care.
And when you are at your lowest,
A Friend is that anchor of support until the end.
For if you have found all this.
You have found—
A Friend

On The Surface

As the drama makes its way,
And it seems never ending,
Stressing one's level to the limit.
Find peace to know what problems that arise
will come to pass.
Sometimes what appears
may not be all what seems.
Sometimes stepping back with an
with an open mind,
with love,
Can work itself out-
On The Surface.

Friends I Know

Fondly I say there are those friends I know-
Whose love is so wonderful to have in one's Life.
Those little things that we sometimes take
for granted, those friends I know—Do!

When those friends I know call me to see if I'm ok.
When those friends I know encourage me to
never give up.

When those friends I know make me laugh
through the sunshine,
and through the rain.
When those friends I know always have a listening ear.

When those friends I know don't mind my imperfections,
Just love me as I am.
When those friends I know take the time to get to know me,
Just to know me.

When those friends I know care,
And offer support and love.
Yes! I'm so glad I have in my life-
Those-
Friends I Know!

Hello Love

Hello Love-
Tell Me! Where can I find you?
I know you're here stacked
away like old books we just
don't seem to want to read anymore.
Hello Love-
I wish you would come back
for us to re-discover again.
I wish I could see you more often.
Hello Love-
Where are you hiding?
Without you, we can just exist,
and eventually if we don't find you,
we'll surely die!
Hello Love-
People don't seem to smile so much
when you're not here.
Compassion seems so far from our reach.

Understanding seems to take up too much of our time.
Kindness has become unique.
Patience is like something so long ago.
Hello Love-
Tell me!-
Where can I find you?

Peace

Sometimes forgiving can be difficult,
Especially when feeling hurt and disappointed.
Sometimes even when the world is unkind,
Being right doesn't hold too much.
Letting go can be such a wonderful feeling,
And the world will seem much nicer.
It's a matter of perspective.
It's a matter how to deal with it
in your mind—in your heart—in your soul.
To let go with no hesitation for the simple
reason to be at-
Peace

Angels Around

There are those who come into our lives to bring a "ray of sunshine"-
just for a little while, and they are gone.

Some come in and out of our lives as a reminder of "God's presence."
Some come to help when we face sorrow, hardship, danger,
disappointment, and distress.

Some come as "guiding posts" to help us find our way.
Some come as "pillars of hope" to give us encouragement.

Some come as "teachers "of many skills to enhance our lives
with knowledge to help us grow.

And some come as "support vendors" to bring us Love.

They all have a reason and purpose in our lives.
They are part of God's House.

They touch our lives in many different ways with His Love.
And some remain forever with us.
For There Are Many-
Angels Around

A Soldier For Peace

In memory of Dr. Martin Luther King Jr.

A Soldier for peace stands mighty and strong.
He stands against racial injustice,
With the love of God-
He Marches On!

A Soldier for peace fights for the civil rights
Of an oppressed people,
For justice and "sweet liberty."
A Soldier fights for their dignity,
For their place,
For equal opportunity.

He leads hundreds on sit-ins,
Protests,
Demonstrations for peace,
Fighting for their freedom,
Yours, and mine.
A Soldier for peace stands tall,
As he fights to end racial discrimination for all time.

A Soldier for peace was shot down.
But his fight for freedom and justice for all-
Remains Strong!
This Soldier For Peace-
A Mighty Warrior!
Brother Martin!
Your Memory Lives On!
Soldiers for peace light the candle of hope to burn brightly in the hearts of all.

A Man Who Is Rich

A Man Who is Rich-
Does not concern himself with success,
And wealth, he gives only the best of himself.

A Man Who is Rich-
Does not care so much about position, or material things.
He values his family, his job, and his friends.

A Man Who is Rich-
Does not forget his responsibilities.
He lives by truth, and integrity.

A Man Who is Rich-
Does not exclude himself from the world around him.
He expands himself to many, and gains the respect of his friends.

A Man Who is Rich-
Does not allow himself to be cynical, bitter, or unkind.
He thrives on positive thinking, he keeps an open mind.

A Man Who Is Rich-
Does not think selfish, or boast about what he does.
He finds fulfillment by doing what is right.
Filling his heart with Love.
For He has all these qualities, and more.
A Man Who is Rich!

What Matters Is Love

What matters is what's in your heart.
For it's all about Love.
Just to keep it with you always.
To see with compassion, mercy,
Tolerance and understanding.
For it's all about Love.

What matters is to be ready to forgive,
Even when the heart is tired and weary,
And to stand no matter your trails, no matter your
Circumstance, no matter your position with the Grace of God.
For it's all about Love.

What matters is to know the respect you give to others,
Will also come back to you.
And to pray at all times, even if you feel there's no
Love around.
For it's all about Love.

What matters is giving always with a humble heart,
Placing less value on things,
And more value into helping others.
For it's all about Love.
Yes!
What matters is what's in your heart.
For it's all about Love!

Didn't You Know?

Didn't you know?-
A little encouragement can go a long way.
For that little encouragement can brighten up someone's day.

Didn't you know?-
That showing respect for others is a good thing to do.
For the respect you give will also come back to you.

Didn't you know?
It's good to take time out to give someone a call,
Or even send a kind note or two.
For that could bring a little sunshine to someone who's feeling blue.

Didn't you know?
Giving a little recognition for a job well done,
Is so important, more than you know.
For doing that, does so much for one's self-worth,
In believing how far they can go.
Didn't you know?
With just a little thoughtfulness you can offer someone
So much.
For those little things can make a difference in the lives
You touch.
Didn't You Know?

Turn The Wheel Around

Don't let negative energy keep going around.
Welcome peace of mind to town.

Pray at all times, even at its worst.
Pray for those who lay on the hurt.

Let positive energy keep going around.
Feel the peace of mind coming to town.

Always "Keep The Faith" and continue to pray.
And let Love be a habit you practice every day.
Just-
Turn The Wheel Around!

The Beauty Of Love

As you love, you live fulfilled.
And as you give love, you encourage
others to give too.
But remember, there're times when love
may not be accepted or received by some.
And sometimes you may feel if it's worth the try.
But just stop and think
as you turn a negative situation
to a positive one,
You'll find much peace, much joy
you can ever imagine when you always
answer to your heart.
Can you ever imagine anything greater?
For that's-
The Beauty Of Love

I Wish To Live Life

I want to receive the Lord's Blessings every day.
I want to be at my best,
Even if I'm at my worst in every way.

I want to hold on to only good feelings in my heart.
I want to move on from disappointments
As I make a new start.

I want to be receptive of change, and not loose me.
I want to always in every situation,
Open my eyes and see.

I want to look back at the past to reflect,
And not feel sorrow.
I want to hold on to hope
As I look forward to tomorrow.

I want to always to "keep the faith"
For dreams to come true.
I want to not remain sad, lonely, and blue.

I want to always let positive thinking
In my life play a vital part.
And-
I want to always have Love in my heart.
For-
I Wish To Live Life!

Could You Sing A Song For Them?

To discover a word different from what you have known,
is to open up doors of understanding, and love.

My Child

My Child may wander off in his own place.
My Child may seem distant,
And he likes his space.

My Child may not like a crowd.
My Child sometimes may be loud.

My Child may not like touch.
My Child may not respond, and speak much.

My Child likes routine.
My Child also likes music, and to sing.

My Child may not run and play like other children do.
My Child likes the Special Olympics, and swimming too!

For there're so many things I can tell you
About my child-
Most Certainly!
But there's just one more thing I got to say-
My Child is everything in the world to me.

My Child!

Invisible

He is different.
Does that make him not important?
No!
For everything you don't understand
About Him,
Are things that only belong to Him?

You see he gets excited at times with a great
amount of energy.
What you don't see is that he sings with a melody
That only belongs to him.

You see him run.
What you don't see is that every year
He participates in Special Olympics-
The 50 yard dash.
It's such an event to see,
And it only belongs to him.

You may see him when he bangs and screams out.
What you don't see he likes to talk to you about
What clothes you may be wearing,
And he'll give you a friendly "hi"-
That only belongs to him.

Invisible to you.
That makes him different!
Because He Has Autism!

Tears

Many times for You I cry tears.
And I go on,
I Cry! I Pray!
To believe someday,
You'll have a place too!
Many times for You I cry tears,
When the world doesn't understand
All about you—I Cry! I Pray!
Hoping you will not waste away
With your beautiful soul,
That some don't always see.
Many times for You I cry tears.
When it's not easy to explain,
Why today you're not doing well,
And you can't express with words
How you feel.
Many times for You I cry tears.
For a great understanding of your
Uniqueness, and worth.
As I accept you exactly as you are—
I Cry! I Pray!
Others will too!

Many times for You I cry tears.
And I go on.
I Cry! I Pray!
To believe someday,
You'll have a place too!
Many times for You I Cry-
Tears.

Changes

Changes are difficult for him to understand.
For he needs time to respond.
Please don't demand!
Changes sometimes puts him
In a place of disarray.
And at times His World is where he wants to stay.
Changes are difficult for him.
And at times,
You don't know what to do.
For if you talk to him.
And find time to pray,
You may find
The answers may come to you.
Changes!
Are difficult for him,
For you,
For me.
Those-
Changes!

Their World

At times you cannot reach them.
And what they have affects their social skills,
And communication.

They also have problems with social interaction.
And some cannot hold a conversation.

They may appear deaf,
And may not respond to you when you talk to them.
And they need advance notice for when you touch them.

Changes in their routine can be difficult for them to understand.
Each of them is unique, and different.
And those who love them do the best they can.

They also have no real fear of dangerous situations.
And all of a sudden they may become overanxious.
And you may not understand them

It is important to learn more about them.
For you can enhance their lives, as well as save them.
For This Is-

Their World.

Building Blocks

Yesterday has come and passed,
Making room for new beginnings,
Making room for today.
We start here—putting the pieces together.
Connecting one by one.
And as we remember each step we took
To get to now,
We see growth.
We see development
Of each one
We teach,
Each one we encourage,
Each one we nurture,
Each one we care for.
Believing each one has potential,
We make room for everyone's
Light to Shine!
Building Blocks!

Could You Sing A Song For Them?

They exist, and you pretend they're not here.
They too have families who love them,
And hold them dear.
Could You Sing A Song For Them?

It may seem as though they may not hear,
And they may walk away.
If you could take the time to know about them,
You may see they have something to say.
Could You Sing A Song For Them?

They may become over anxious at times
for no apparent reason.
They have a difficult time understanding
change in routine.
Could You Sing A Song For Them?

And they may not be able to communicate
like you and me.
They may not tend to one task for too long.
For this is their Disability.
Could You Sing A Song For Them?

Their Disability is-
Autism,
Asperger's Syndrome,
Autism Spectrum Disorder.
And there are other terms too.
Could you give them a chance?
For they live here just like me and you.
Could You Sing A Song For Them?

The Puzzle

If we could put the pieces together,
Let's start by learning all about it.
That would be a wonderful thing
We could do for each one who has it.

Let's open up our hearts.
And with the challenges,
Let's teach them how to live in our world.
For each of them is an individual.
And let's provide for each individual need.

Let's make sure each child and adult is not overlooked.
Let's provide a more productive future
For each and every one of them.
Let's enhance their growth and development
By providing them a better quality of life.
Each one is a person,
God Loves them,
They all have their place.
It will take much Awareness,
And most of all our Understanding.
Autism!
We Can Solve-
The Puzzle.

Hope

Always with faith, all things are possible on each given day.

This Day Today

This day today,
I took a moment to breathe,
To laugh,
And to smile.

This day today,
I saw hope through the disappointments.
To stay always encouraged.

This day today,
I focused on the goodness.
To know all gets better if one believes.

This day today,
I practiced the act of Faith,
To keep going,
To never give up.

This day today,
I took a moment to breathe,
To laugh,
To smile,
And to Pray!
This Day Today!

Foundation

Rebuilding—starting over
with dreams set in motion,
there's a life to get back.
Reorganizing and going another direction,
there's a feeling this time it will be different,
this time it will be better.
And as one storm has passed,
then before you know comes another one.
But this time it's different.
And as the peace within you overflows,
prosperity is not far off.
Rebuilding—starting over
with dreams set in motion,
there's a life to get back.
My Life!

Prosperity

For now, needs are to be met.
For now,
I pray for prosperity.
This moment,
I wish for prosperity.
And as I start again in a new phase
of my life,
I can only hold on to hope.

For this is my challenge.
And tomorrow all this will change.
Prosperity will be soon.
At this moment,
At this hard place,
I Hold On!

As You're Going Through

I can worry when things aren't what
they should be.
I can be stressed every minute,
Every hour of the day when problems arise.

I can feel my heart with anxiety when it seems
it's not getting better.
I can take my stress level to another level,
Angry, bitter and just feeling not so good at all.
Yet, I can see the sunshine through it all.
He's taught me that so very much.
And as I believe tomorrow will be better
than I can ever imagine,
I'm at peace.

The Sunshine

When your day seems cloudy and gray.
Pray the Lord will take your blues away.
Just Look for the Sunshine

And before you know it, what's troubling you.
Will start to go away, and you're no longer blue.
Just Look for the Sunshine

For you decide how you live for whatever way
you choose.
And if your way of living is positive,
you have nothing to loose.
Just Look for the Sunshine

For if you wear a smile, and not a frown,
You'll find many of life's challenges will not get you down.
Just Look for the Sunshine

Remember to keep the love in your heart.
For staying positive is the most important part.
Just Look For-
The Sunshine!

In Due Season

When I think about all the blessings
He brings.
When I think about His Grace—His Love,
I can only stay where he wants me to be.
I cannot doubt him,
No matter what,
No matter the challenges.
And when the storms come,
And it seems as though they will not pass,
I look up to Him to know
He's my help,
He's my friend.
And whatever my desires,
I know He will grant.
Yes,
Always-
In Due Season

Through And Beyond The Storm

See the sun as the storm comes.
He brings hope through it all.
Hold on to it always.
Trust in Him.
He's always there.
Sometimes Life can bring
Many challenges.
Sometimes all at once.
And whatever comes to be,
Know it will pass.
Hold on,
And Pray.
For as the Storm comes,
Know He'll always be there-
Through And Beyond!

A Soldier's Song

I pray for you who fights in a distant land far from home.
I pray as God brings you back home.

Pray for the soldier who fights in a
Distant land far from home,
Whose life is uncertain at every turn.

Pray for the soldier facing the gun,
In a world in turmoil and despair.
Pray for him—for her as they fight
For honor and love for country.

Pray for as long as the soldier endures a war
For how ever long it may be.
Pray for the families and friends
Who longs for a soldier's safe return.

Pray for peace to come as the soldier
Endures each minute, each hour,
Each day to live, just to live.

Pray for the soldier who fights in a
Distant land far from home,
As God brings each one Home.

The Sun Still Shines In The Morning

The dark clouds came, and have passed. We remember, and yet
We can see—The Sun Still Shines In The Morning.

We ask: Will it ever be the same again?
And can we still see the sun still shines in the morning?
For one September morning, a dark cloud covered
the skies of Manhattan in the New City.
The Towers that stood so tall came down leaving
A heavy smoke and its memory.
Two planes crashed into its center,
leaving much destruction, and despair.

Many lives were taken, and there were some lives
spared to tell of its tragic death.
We mourned, and we still mourn like a weight of
despair that lies so deep in our hearts—we're numb.
Like a passing of a love one we go on.
The fire still burns as a reminder,
And the dark cloud has been lifted,
And we go on.

Now we're at war, holding on to hope it will never
come again,
And we go on.
We pray, and as we hold on to hope,
We can see miraculous wonders of God's Love,
And the fire still burns,
And we go on.
We ask: Will it ever be the same again?
But if we look around the corner, we'll see-
The Sun Still Shines In The Morning!

As Tomorrow Comes

Hope may seem difficult to hold on to.
And whatever challenges you may
Experience at the present day,
Know it's a temporary thing.
For today may not be your tomorrow.

Hold on to the Hope when it seems
Difficult to do so.
Just Hold On.
And believe the sun will rise again.
Yes!
The sun will rise-
As Tomorrow Comes.

My Prayer For You

I pray His Love will shower upon you each day.
May his arms surround you,
To encourage you through your travels,
To comfort you when you need a friend,
To guide and sustain you through the most
difficult times.

May you find joy as the morning comes.
And may it stay with you as the sun goes down,
To hold you to the new day at the break of dawn.

I pray His Love shower upon you each day
of your life.
May His Love be with you always.

Where The Grass Is Green

There has to be a place—Where the Grass is Green,
Where love is—always Love.

There has to be a place—Where the Grass is Green,
Where I can be me,
And not concern myself if it's ok.

There has to be a place—Where the Grass is Green,
Where patience lies,
And positive energy spreads in every direction.

There has to be a place—Where the Grass is Green,
Where there's no fear to live each day,
And to trust is common practice.

There has to be a place—Where the Grass is Green,
Where the quality of life is abundant,
And working hard has more value.

There has to be a place—Where the Grass is Green,
Where war is just a distant memory of
Yesterday,
And peace is something we don't have to
Dream about.

There has to be a place—Where the Grass is Green,
Where Love keeps growing,
Crushing hate to the ground.

There has to be a place—Where the Grass is Green,
Where love is—always Love.
There has to be a place-
Where The Grass Is Green.

Hope

Giving up is surrender to no place.
When all seems lost, holding on
brings you one step closer to the promise.
And as you believe each day is a new day,
your trials can be your triumph.
Just believe that it all gets better,
no matter your circumstance,
no matter what you go through.
Believe what is now can change tomorrow.
Believe with Faith.
And always hold on to-
Hope.

Morning

Yesterday has come and gone.
Tomorrow brings promise,
And always hope.
And for now,
I'm doing alright.
Yes! I'm doing just fine.
And each breath I take,
It's Good.
Yes! It's All Good!
Hello-
Morning!

Blessings

To be inspired is to be taken to a place where only heaven lives.

Autumn

Leaves from the trees turn red, orange, yellow, and brown.
They're no longer green.
With its cool mornings, warm afternoons,
And as the leaves fall from the trees,
Autumn has a beauty to be seen.

As school starts for some,
And football is the major sport of the season,
The nights become brisk, and cool.
And winter is just around the corner as we know.
And as winter approaches,
We start to ask the question: "Will we get much snow?"

There's the holiday Halloween, when children,
And adults dress up as characters in disguise of their own desire,
In late October for "trick or treat" for the night.
And with the holiday Thanksgiving,
A time for family and friends
Gather together for a wonderful feast,
With love for one another, such a wonderful sight.

Autumn! Autumn! Autumn!
With summer behind—winter ahead.
There's not much more to be said.
For this is the season we call-
Autumn!

The Fall

Long hot days of summer past.
Cool mornings,
Warm afternoons,
And the evening breeze creeps in.
Leaves falling,
Smothering the ground,
As the cool breeze blows.

Warm delicious apple pie,
Caramel apples,
And hot soups to eat.
Hot cocoa,
Hot coffee,
Hot tea to drink.
Football games to watch,
And play.
Days grow short,
And the nights grow longer.
The prelude to winter.
Long hot days of summer past.
The Fall

The Winds Of The Seasons

The winds of winter,
Cold and yet warm in thoughts.
The falling of snow,
How beautiful you are.
While Christmas comes
With the joy of giving,
And the reminder of what
It's all about-
A child born in a manger-
The light of the world,
Bringing Hope,
As the New Year approaches.
And before you know,
Spring is here ready to take its place.
Trees grow,
Flowers blossom all around.
Warm winds fill the air,
And soon summer comes to life, sunshine,
Beautiful long days,
And wonderful exciting nights.
Leading into the fall, as leaves start to fall,
And the air becomes cool again.

The Winds of the Seasons
Are the Circles of life.
All have their beauty.
All have their purpose.
How beautiful they are-
The Winds Of The Seasons

A Day In Winter

It's a day in winter of a New Year.
The snow falls here and there.
Covering the branches so bare.
And the coming of spring draws near.

Inches of snow just a few.
Paints a picture of a lovely winter frost.
For on this day,
Cold and brisk,
The air so fresh and new,
Comes the beauty of winter,
As it passes through.
It's a Day in Winter-
So Nice!

Walking In The Rain

The pouring of raindrops coming down,
Brings a soothing to your soul.
And as you gather your thoughts,
There's peace within.

The sun shines within you.
Such therapy for the soul.
Walking In The Rain

Clouds For Today

The clouds tell us where we're going,
And the rain which is constant relays so much.
Will the sun come-
Oh Yes!
It will tomorrow.
Spring doesn't seem like spring at this moment.
The seasons will change a bit.
For this has been foretold.
But will the sun shine.
Oh Yes!
It will tomorrow.
Know this will pass.
Yes, it will.
The clouds don't have to cloud our hearts,
And the rain doesn't have to make us blue.
Remember the sun can shine,
Even when you don't see it.
The Sun can shine in You!
For right now, there are just-
Clouds For Today!

The Coming Of Spring

Winter breeze still lingers on.
And yet, winter soon will be gone.

Soon there'll be no more snow.
Trees will start to turn green,
As plants start to grow.

Raindrops, Raindrops,
Will fall here and there.
And flowers will blossom everywhere.

Visions of daffodils,
Tulips,
Pink and red roses,
Blossoming all around.
The birds chirping,
Such a beautiful sound.

As the days become longer,
Comes many wonderful things to do.
Jogging,
Bicycle riding,
Even walks in the park too!
More rides to view the countryside in the car.
Soon warm and lovely weather is not far.

The beauty of April, May, and June.
For its arrival will be soon.
The Coming Of Spring!

A Summer Breeze

I wait for long days, short nights.
I wait for weather so nice,
I can feel the breeze upon me.
I wait for vacation in different
Places never have known,
Only dreamed.
I wait for family gatherings, barbecues,
Picnics, and much more.
I wait as nightfall comes,
Hopeful what each new day will bring.
I wait as I say "Good Night" to
Loved ones I hold dear more assured.
I wait for-
A Summer Breeze.

Reminders

There'll always be reminders
of what's long past.
Surfacing over and over again.
Reflections of distant memories,
And what is now.
Reminders as one's life changes,
Growth can be a challenge,
And the will to survive is a test
of the spirit.
Reminders to say it's ok
to look back without living there.
To move on, and to let go.
Reminders to understand what
was, is not now to live,
And always to learn.
While the pages of life's experiences
Continue to turn.
There'll always be-
Reminders

Letting Go

Cleansing in one's soul.
Peace,
And serenity flows.
Hurt,
And pain released.
Your heart at peace.
Love steps in,
As you surrender it to Him.
Letting Go!

Whirlwind

In a whirlwind spinning
out of control.
Finally stepping back
to see what direction
you're taking.
Is it good,
Is it right.
Understanding what is meant to be.
Revaluating all of it since it started,
And where it is now.
Then to realize for self,
That Acceptance is Peace.

Needing Space

Need some space,
Just for a little while.
Trying to find my way to
where I need to be.
Only needing time with my thoughts.
Yes, my thoughts.
So I can breathe, laugh, and smile again.
Needing Space

The Morning Sun

Revelations came to me
At the break of dawn.
Realizing many things.
Looking over my life,
How it has been,
Where I am now,
And where I am going.
Letting go of issues from others,
Issues I have, I'm facing
What I can't change.
And I'm moving forward to a new change.
My healing begins.
And I can see clear,
As I see-
The Morning Sun

A Time, A Season, And Always Love

I pray more than ever now,
At a time where perceptions,
And what's on the surface
Has more weight, I pray for Love.

I pray for a revaluation of thoughts
To see love, and believe in it so.

For each season,
Each winter as the snow falls,
Each spring as the flowers blossom,
And the trees grow,
Each summer as more sunny
And warm days appear,
Each fall as the leaves fall,
And the cool winds fill the air,
I pray for each time,
Each season for love to stay.

I pray for a time where the act of trust,
And faith in humankind becomes more present,
Especially now.

I pray for Love to stay always,
Yes! Always!

I Pray for-
A Time, A Season, And Always Love.

Blessings

The sun shining all the time
Life through devastation
Seeing an unborn child
Prayers answered over and over again
Giving life back
Finding peace
Children laughing and playing
A smile
Being in Love
Seizing the moments
The Love of a mother
A father's joy
A child's gift
Family gatherings
Friendship
Seeing an old friend
Unexpected presents
A bouquet of flowers
Pink roses
Snow on Christmas Day
Spring in Washington DC
A rainbow after the rain

Summer breezes
A thank you for no reason
Encouragement
Fulfillment
Inspirational messages
A pat on the back
A Hug
Congratulations
A listening ear
A helping hand
An understanding heart
Love-
Blessings!

Home

Balancing it all together,
What makes sense is the
Purpose of why I'm here.
Where I am meant to be-
At peace always,
In my soul always.
And yes,
Love I find everywhere.
While other things come and go,
Love never dies!
I see the morning sun,
I start a new day.
And it's all because of you.
You have given me new life.
More greater than I can ever imagine.
It never left me.
Though at times I've moved away from it.
And this is where I will stay.
So glad I found my way back—here.
Dear Lord!
So glad I'm-
Home.

Blessings From Doris Washington

Live each day with God's blessings and love.
Remember He watches from above.
Cherish each moment you live.
Never stop believing in miracles,
And of yourself give.
Take time to help someone as best as you can.
Remember God blesses you with at least one friend.
Hold on to the many good things.
And always welcome the Lord's Blessings.
Be At Peace!
Be At Peace!
Be At Peace!

Faith, Hope & Love

Faith never says "what if" it says for sure. It inspires one's deepest desires to believe all things are possible.

Hope is holding on to the sunshine on each given day. And to believe in today and tomorrow.

Love inspires with positive energy. It hears, listens, and always answers to the heart. For there's nothing more beautiful than love.

LaVergne, TN USA
20 November 2010

205727LV00003B/100/P